Michiana Monologues 2014:
City of Women

Edited by Angie Rice

Indiana University South Bend

Acknowledgments:

This book would not be possible without the dozens of people who volunteered their time, energy, and vision to this year's production of the Michiana Monologues. In particular, we wish to thank the hard-working and insightful 2014 editorial board: Sara Curtis, Jessica Kaiser, Rhonda Redman, Catherine Hebert, Shelly Overgaard, Jill Longnecker, April Lidinsky, Rachel Berryman, Sam Arguinzoni, Georgette Hood, and Kris Robinson. Danica Duensing continues to design and manage our website. Thanks to our new co-directors, Cheri Gray and Shelly Overgaard, for their leadership. Many thanks to Lynn Langston who headed up our oral story-collection group. Thank you to Ken Smith and David James of Wolfson Press for production support. Thanks to Brikayla Hardy for being president of the student group this year, and to Fredd Overgaard for volunteering to design the cover. And last but not least, we would like to express our deepest gratitude and appreciation to the many people who continue to help us with logistics and support so that we can bring this production to an expanding number of venues on campus and in the community.

ISBN 978-1-939674-03-6

Printed in the U.S.A.

Table of Contents

Introduction

"Activism is the rent I pay for living on this planet"
~ Alice Walker

We think of this as our "lucky 7th year" of Michiana Monologues activism–
and activism is what the Monologues is, indeed, in the form of story-
collecting, reading, writing, and theater. These are the tools we use–and YOU
use–to change the world for the better. Art has power, and by holding this
book and reading these words, you are part of this exciting experience of
using creativity as a tool for social change.

Many of you might already know the "herstory" of the Michiana
Monologues. For many years at Indiana University South Bend, a student
club produced Eve Ensler's ground-breaking feminist play, *The Vagina
Monologues*. The production brings to light many aspects of women's
experiences that are rarely spoken of, and so it served as a means to enlighten
and entertain the audience. The play was a campus success, but in 2008,
we decided to shift to a different kind of production, a local production,
featuring stories written by women in our own community. We were betting
that stories written by the women right here in Michiana would be just as
inspiring, funny, difficult, complicated, and moving as those in Ensler's play.
Happily, we were right. Since then, we have solicited stories annually from
women in the greater Michiana area, and every year we are amazed and
enriched by the talent of local writers and the breadth of experiences they
capture on the page.

Michiana Monologues has three purposes: to enlighten our community about
the real experiences of women's lives; to entertain audiences and readers;
to raise money for crucial organizations working to end violence in our
community. Each year, thousands of audience members gather to hear the
production and purchase the books, t-shirts, and bid on silent auction items
donated by people in the community who share our vision of using art as a
tool to end violence.

The stories featured in Michiana Monologues are gathered year-round
through our website, www.michianamonologues.org, which features tips
for "telling big stories in small spaces," as we like to say. We offer writing

workshops all over the community, designed to invite women to see their stories as worth telling, worth hearing, and worth sharing. This year, we expanded our reach by gathering stories orally as well, with recording equipment at sound booths during Art Beat and First Fridays events in South Bend and other area locations. We also offer writing workshops to interested groups. We are always inspired by the bravery of women who tell a story for the first time, and are often surprised by the rush of shared feeling in the room: "You, too? I thought I was the only one ..." In that moment, a monologue becomes a dialogue, and a dialogue becomes a conversation that can change a community.

We suspect you might feel that rush of shared feeling when you read many of the stories in this collection. This year, our collection includes experiences such as finding empowerment through playing a brass instrument, coming to terms with an aging body, falling in love (and out of love) with a damaged person, and lessons learned while being incarcerated, or loving someone who is. You will also hear stories that celebrate parts of the body that are often reviled, and stories that approach sexuality from fresh–and perhaps quite surprising–perspectives. Barbie makes an appearance, as do commercials for cleaning products (featuring...you guessed it...women!), and so do those shirts that declare D.A.D.D. (Dads Against Daughters Dating). You will read about open-minded parents, tender friends, and many different perspectives on motherhood. You will also learn what it means to have a "Two Spirit" identity, and to feel like one's body should not determine who gets to carry a "girl card." In these varied voices, you'll hear that violence and healing take many different forms, and that anger and humor often weave together in acts of survival. Mostly, we suspect you will be struck–as we are–by the resilience and optimism of these writers. We hope you are inspired to respond.

This volume contains more stories than we were able to bring to the stage this year. We regret that we do not have space even in this book to include every submission we received. If your story does not appear on stage or in this book, it is not because it wasn't powerful, moving, or unique. We congratulate everyone who submitted a monologue for consideration; the act of writing–of telling the truth–is a radical act. Thank you for taking that courageous leap.

This community chorus does more than enlighten and entertain us; these voices raise money for crucial organizations that work to improve our community. This year our expanded beneficiary list includes: SOS of the Family Justice Center, St. Margaret's House, YWCA of North Central Indiana, Elkhart County Women's Shelter, GLBT Resource Center of Michiana, The Young Moms' Self-Sufficiency Program of the Youth Service Bureau, Planned Parenthood of Indiana and Kentucky, Maple City Health Care Center, and Indiana Legal Services, Inc.

We hope these powerful stories stay with you. We hope you see them, as we do, as activism of the kind that writer Alice Walker calls for–as a way to "pay rent" to a world full of problems, but even more full of potential. When you read these stories, support those who tell them, and are moved to respond, you are an activist, too. Thank you.

}{

Heart of Brass

Brassy women were a feature of my childhood. Parents, relations, teachers, scout leaders, coaches, friends' moms—they were always on me and the other girls my age that we could be whatever we wanted. It was the 90s, and the liberal feminist adults in my life were bent on driving that fact home. You can be anything you want to be. Nothing is closed to you. Doesn't matter what other people think; follow your passions.

Except that I didn't really have any passions. Neither did I have any particular ambitions planned out for my life on that fateful night in fifth grade, when my parents took me to the district-wide band instrument-testing night at the high school gym, and I was told that I should definitely play the trumpet.

The trumpet? Seriously?

Girls don't play trumpet. Nobody plays trumpet! Nobody but guys with weasely moustaches and thin lips, and that black guy Satch something. Whatever. Who cares? I'm only doing band because my friends are doing it.

How little I knew.

For example, I didn't know that when you put 600 band kids from six elementary schools and one high school into one gym, that absolutely every surface will resonate as though touched by God, that you can see the air itself quiver and dance in front of you, and the parents in the stands will weep openly as you approach the climax of the theme from Jurassic Park.

I couldn't anticipate that moment in junior high, being called upon to stand and bow at the end of my first solo, and feeling for the first time, in any context, an opioid rush of pride and joy in my own achievements, nor that that feeling never goes away.

I would never have guessed that my high school years would find me at marching band rehearsal on a cold November morning perfecting a look of mingled nausea, disbelief and resignation as the rest of the trumpet section, bored and ignored, created a small lake of their own spit and proceed to pick up and hoist the smallest section member over it like Superman. I learned how to lead them, and other trumpet sections. I learned how to hold my own in a pack of men and command their respect.

But most of all, I didn't know that we don't get to choose our passions. In Harry Potter, the wand chooses the wizard, and in life, the obsession chooses the mind that's opened enough to let it in. I didn't choose to play the trumpet; the trumpet chose me. And though that moment wasn't underscored with flying sparks or the music of John Williams, it set events into motion that would shape the rest of my life.

Music has transfigured me. Before, I was a quiet girl with a lot of daydreams and little direction in life. The brassy women who raised me and pushed me through life did their best, but the trumpet's call spoke to me with greater eloquence. When I pick up the horn, I am transformed. I am confident, and I am driven. This is as true today as it was when I first learned it at age fourteen. And after fifteen years of pursuing music, through passion and burnout, through success and failure and success again, the greatest lesson I have learned is this: If I am to have fire in my heart and iron in my spine, I must have brass in my hands.

Four Brothers

I grew up with four brothers. That may sound like a curse, but it was really a blessing. We lived in the country for most of my childhood and learned to rely on each other for entertainment.

We moved to South Bend just before my sophomore year of high school. It was Fall and I was cleaning house and doing laundry while my brothers were out playing with neighborhood kids. Typical, right??

My youngest brother came back to the house to ask me to come out to play football with them and the neighborhood kids. I told him I had too much work to do, but he begged me to come out. It seemed they would be short on one side.

I finally relented and went out to the side street where the game was to be played. We all stood there waiting to see who got picked for which team. When my brother picked me, the guys on the other team just snickered. And I knew what they were thinking. Your sister?? You picked the only girl? TeeHee!

We got under way and the other team had the ball. When the guy ran to me, I reached out and tackled him. He jumped up sputtering and said, "She tackled me. She tackled me." I looked at him and said, "Aren't we playing tackle football?" He looked at me and said, "But you're a girl!"

I looked over at my two older brothers and they are laughing their asses off! And it hit me. They had set the kid up. They knew he was a know-it-all and chauvinist, and they had faith that I could take him out in the game! I had never been more proud to be their sister, and I know that this helped me to be a strong and independent woman.

Growing up with all those brothers was definitely a blessing!!

Special Delivery: The Lies That Mattel Told Me!

Nothing inside
Just plain old plastic
The frustration
Agonizing pain of waiting
To see the package that Ken
Had waiting for me
You see an 8 year-old girl wants to
Explore and learn
Curiosity sure did kill this cat
I waited for months deciding when to peek
I was so curious because well I wanted to know
Is it pink, tan, solid, or hairy?
What is down there?!
Does it look like me?
Is it like mine?
I needed to know
But I couldn't ask
Because girls shouldn't ask about special deliveries.
But I had to know what surprise Ken was hiding!
I mean because of course it was a surprise, it had to be
Because I was so ashamed to peek inside and even more ashamed to ask
about it
Well the day finally came and I was ready.
My heart was racing
I would find out what Ken had
So I started to peek
I closed it up
Not yet; I'm not ready
And I went in again to peek at Ken
NOTHING! Not a thing was inside!
Ken looked like Barbie and I knew this couldn't be right
No way there are separate bathrooms if we all look the same!
Mattel Lied!

Bloody Hell

After dropping my pants in the kitchen in front of my mom for the fifth time, we both agreed I had officially gotten my first period. Two spots of dark red-brown on a pad the size of a telephone book meant that I was now a woman.

What does that mean?

If it means calling all your friends and bragging about being the first to get your period, then I was now a woman. FYI, I plan on calling all my friends and bragging about being the first to start menopause too, because that means NO MORE PERIODS. The circle will be complete.

Being the first in your group of friends to get your period really isn't all that great. You feel cool for about a day, and then the cramps kick in. And when you're in the fifth grade, it's weird. My mom made me keep a pad in a little zipper case that I snapped into the back of my Trapper Keeper. "Just in case" she said. Because pad dispensers aren't readily available in elementary schools.

One day my friend (who soon became my enemy) was flipping through my Trapper, admiring my Lisa Frank folders, when she came upon my little zipper case. Curious, she unzipped it, pulled out the pad, then dropped it like it was a turd or something. She shrieked and kicked it down the hall. My secret pad was now the ball in an impromptu game of soccer, as other kids joined in, kicking it away. I didn't feel so important and grown-up anymore. I wanted to go back to playing with G. I. Joe guys in the dirt. I didn't want to worry about girls sticking pads on my locker. This puberty thing sure did suck.

Probably the worst experience I had with Auntie Flo was at a slumber party. Even at twelve I had a very heavy flow and changed pads every few hours. Oh, and tampons? Hell no. Sticking a wad of cotton up my hoo-ha was out of the question. I'd rather sit on a mattress in my pants.

Anyway, I had a cute pair of new pink shortie pajamas to show off at said slumber party. And show off I did. In the morning, I awoke to screams. I had kicked off my sleeping bag in my sleep and my left side was exposed. I had been sleeping on my back. I had not gotten up to go to the bathroom all night long. Do we see where this is going?

My friends thought I had been stabbed in my sleep because I was lying in a pool of blood. Those horror movies we watched last night didn't help the hysteria. The screaming woke my friend's dad, who came into the basement, saw blood, turned green, then went upstairs to get my friend's mom. She immediately understood and took care of me, god bless her.

I still owe you, Mrs. K!

Chesty

I am a 38 DD. My breasts are the first characteristic that people notice. And sometimes, they are the only characteristic people notice.

Let me tell you how things got started. I must have been eight or nine. I noticed that my chest hurt after a stray elbow grazed me during some good-natured rough housing. I told my older brother, "Look, it hurts when I push here. Try it." He looked away from me for a long moment. Then he said, "If it hurts, don't do it." Later that summer, before school started, my mom suggested I try on some sports bras. And things really took off from there. By sixth grade, I was wearing my mom's hand-me-down bras.

Here are some things that my breasts caused to happen to me:

In sixth grade, when I was eleven, I found out my boyfriend only liked me because of my giant boobs. I became instantly suspicious of male attention.

I HATED gym class because my boobs bounced around and everyone watched.

I would cry silently but profusely in bed at night and fantasize about cutting them off my body with a kitchen knife.

At fifteen, I was approached by a twenty-something man who asked for my phone number and if we could hang out. He asked how old I was as an after thought. When I turned him down, he then told me I looked much older, said he was sorry, and walked away.

When I was eighteen, attending Purdue University, I met my friend's roommate who had secretly had a breast enlargement before classes started. She lit up at my presence, hugged me three times in a row, and then eventually reached out and felt me up to see how real ones felt. And this is actually a trend. I can't tell you how many times women have grabbed at me or asked to feel my breasts to compare to their own.

Young men would walk up to me out of nowhere and ask for my phone number, then retreat in disgust and call me a bitch because I didn't respond the way they had anticipated. Men hollered and cat-called me on campus. Every. Single. Day. Like my breast size suddenly gave everyone permission to engage me sexually. Meanwhile, women were saying how envious they were and how lucky I was to have such large breasts.

When I talked about getting a reduction, women lamented the troubles it would cause to breast feeding and how devastated I would be. They effectively scared me away from the idea for years.

At twenty-one, going out to bars with friends was a nightmare. Men totally unembarrassed ogled and stared, making gestures and noises and crying out. They would pester and harass us. They would get angry when they realized my breast size did not mean I was easy to sack.

I was too afraid of the inevitable harassment to exercise. I started to put on weight. My breasts got larger. Exercising got harder.

When I stand for too long, my back and shoulders ache. When I lie down to ease the pressure, my breasts crowd up to touch my chin. My breasts impede the movement of my arms. The seat belt in my car always slides up to my neck.

Good bras are expensive and hard to find. My bra straps dig into my shoulders where there is a permanent dent in my flesh. Not wearing a bra is too uncomfortable, so I wear one almost twenty-four hours a day.

I can't wear button up shirts, they gap between the buttons. Even the most modest v-neck flashes ample cleavage. Wearing a crew neck makes my breasts look larger. I have to buy clothes too large to fit my breasts. I look dumpy a lot. I can only wear simple cotton tops.

People feel free to publicly discuss my breasts because I dont have the option of hiding them.

At work, when I know I will be with certain clients, I have to make ultra conservative wardrobe choices to minimize the amount of attention they will give my breasts.

I dream about getting a reduction some day soon. But a breast reduction costs well over $6,000. I don't have insurance, and insurance often doesn't cover it anyway. I don't make enough money to save for the surgery. I have no idea when I will be able to afford it. Or if I ever will.

I dream of the day I will be able to take a run. I dream of the day I can wear a button up shirt. I dream of the day my breasts don't choke me when I'm lying down. I dream of the day people notice my face first.

I think I have a pretty face and I'm funny, too. I wish that's what people noticed about me first.

Can You See Me?

Let's play a game. I am going to describe myself, and I want you to try to imagine me, the kind of person I am. I am a mother. I have a four year old daughter who I cherish more than life. We cook dinner together every night and I make her vegan blueberry pancakes for breakfast at least twice a week. I read her a bedtime story, or two, if she has her way, every night. We have living room picnics, play with letter flashcards and have bubble fights in the bath tub. I am lucky to have her and dedicated to being the very best mother I can be. Can you see me yet?

I am a student. I work hard and forego sleep to maintain a 3.9 GPA. I present at conferences and have had my research published. I want to graduate with honors and go to law school, so I can help people who haven't had a fair shake in life. I want, with my whole soul, to make a difference in this world. Am I getting clearer?

I wear my heart on my sleeve. I am so sensitive that I am a vegetarian, because seeing anyone suffer, even an animal, makes me feel as if my heart is being ripped apart. Sometimes I lay awake at night sobbing because of all the pain in the world that I can't fix. I am a loyal friend, one who is always there with a shoulder, a meal or a couch if need be. I protect the ones I love with a ferociousness that is sometimes scary. How do I look now?

Now that you're starting to see me, let me say this: I am a slut, or at least society would define me as one. I have had twosomes, threesomes, and a single foursome. I have partner swapped, had sex in public, and my partners are nearing the triple digit mark. I love sex. I revel in the feel and taste of a new partner. I have slept with people whose last names I will never know, and I feel no regret for any of it. How do I look to you now?

Society would have you believe that I am deviant, that I am solely defined by these sexual acts, that somehow because I enjoy my body, and the bodies of my lovers, that I am less of a mother, that my scholastic achievements mean nothing compared to whether missionary or doggy style is my position of choice.

Does it make it better if I tell you that my daughter has not met a single one of my sexual partners? Would you judge me less? Or if I told you that sometimes I am celibate for entire academic semesters because I don't want anything to interfere with my studies? Am I redeemed?

I am a mother, a student, a friend, an overachiever, a do-gooder, and a slut. Can you see ME now?

Voice

When I was young, about fourteen or fifteen years old, I was learning gymnastics from a friend of mine. My parents couldn't afford lessons, but a friend of mine took lessons, and I liked to practice by myself. I also loved to go for walks on the beach between five and six o'clock, before dinner, when it was kind of quiet and the light was really beautiful. So one evening I put on my bikini and put a big man's shirt over it, so proud that I'd gotten this shirt at a thrift store, and I walked alone and just enjoyed the beautiful air of the evening by the seashore. I got to where I thought was a relatively isolated area so no one could see me make any mistakes, and I could just practice my handsprings or whatever I was trying to do.

I did a few cartwheels just for fun. Little did I know that there was a group of guys in the bushes nearby. I was just hearing the ocean, and I was doing my gymnastics in the sand, kind of lost in my own world.

I heard footsteps behind me. Running fast. And I thought, "Oh no, I wonder if there's a big dog behind me," because I was afraid of dogs. So I remembered the advice that people had given me, just keep on doing what you're doing, don't look at them, just keep on going, and I did. Then I felt my bikini bottoms being ripped from my body. I was just so shocked.

I–I completely lost my voice.

A young man in jeans and cowboy boots, buzz-cut haircut, was running away from me as fast as he'd run up to me, and his friends were laughing in the bushes. And I pulled my bottoms up real fast, and I was shaking, and I turned around to walk home, and I looked around. Was there anyone else around?

And I saw a couple, not too far away, and I walked towards them, and then…I tried to speak, and I–I still–I couldn't talk to them. I walked home. And I didn't tell my mother, because I thought, "She'll never let me go to the beach again, or do anything by myself." And I didn't think about my bathing suit.

She found it later, and it was completely ripped. All the lining had been ripped out, like, by fingers.

And she said, "What happened to your bathing suit?" and I said, "Oh, um, I guess it's getting old. I can sew it if you want me to, or we can get a new one."

She said, "Well, I can sew it for you."

When I told my best friend about it she said, "Why didn't you yell at him, that son of a bitch?"

I said, "I couldn't. I couldn't yell. I wish—I thought about all kinds of things I could have said, but…I had no voice."

Many years later, I was walking home to my apartment, which was in a nice, quiet neighborhood. I had gone to get milk at the corner store. And I noticed there was a man following me, and it started to make me a little nervous when I got towards the door. I really got a bad feeling the last part of my walk, and I went in the glass door, and I closed it, and there he was, outside the door, with his…with his coat open, his penis exposed, and he was… jacking off.

And I looked at him, and I said, "You ought to be ashamed of yourself!" I said, "There are young children in this house, and you are not respecting me, and you better get out of here!"

And he did. He left.

And I was so glad–I was so grateful–that I had found my voice.

Tire

"With most people you can pinch an inch, but with Sally you can grab a slab," my dad said.

I was nine.

"We'll call you Tire, because Goodyear makes tires as well as blimps, and you look like the Goodyear blimp," my dad said.

I was eleven. He laughed.

"What's that nasty thing on your face?" my dad asked, after I had given myself a chemical burn trying to get rid of a zit.

"It's a good thing you wear glasses because it makes your nose look smaller."

"What did you do to make him leave you?"

"Did you cut your hair with a weed whacker?"

You would think the comments would roll off my back by now, but they don't. They stick like tiny quills in my skin. I'm half porcupine by now. My dad isn't a bad person nor a bad father. He's just insensitive.

I'm not making excuses–he's said some pretty fucking hurtful things. And I'm sure there are still ones to come.

My husband threatened him on our wedding day and told him he had better tell me I was beautiful and he was proud of me. He did. I kinda believed it. I know he's proud of me. I'm an accomplished musician, I'm highly educated, I'm active in the community. But he's only proud of things he can brag about.

"That's my daughter, she plays the piano so well because I bought all her music."

"I paid for the acting lessons when she was a kid and that's why she's up there now."

"I put you through college, that's why you have a good job."

I love my dad. Our relationship now is better than ever. There have been times when I didn't talk to him for days, weeks, months, almost years. But life's too short, and he is my dad.

I can depend on him. He continues to teach me things. We watch Notre Dame games together and swear at the tv in unison. We help each other do yardwork. He's amazingly intelligent and I love having conversations with him on topics from politics to The Big Bang Theory (the tv show, not the physics thing). The good definitely outweighs the bad. Ha ha. I said weighs.

Words hurt. But so does holding a grudge.

Beautiful Body

It houses a soul that often thinks of others first.
It has a mind that encompasses new ideas until proven faulty or not valuable.
It has a smile that passes to its sisters in a hug.
It carries itself with grandeur in all situations.
It considers itself to be sexy and loved beyond comparison.
It is brave yet humble.
It challenges itself to personal growth.
It seeks education.
It longs to understand as well as be understood.
It conveys care and concern; power and dignity; leadership and following.
It is resilient in trials.
It knows weeping in adversity is not weakness, but a way to express concern.
It loves unconditionally and without prejudice.
It is not to be controlled.
It recognizes the difference between love and abuse.
It cannot be measured by a clothing rack, sideways glance, whistle, or gaze.
It can only be measured by the confidence of she who dwells within.

A beautiful body knows her strength.
A beautiful body embraces herself as lovely and divine in all circumstances.
A beautiful body gives no regard to external pressure, coercion, or structure.
A beautiful body lives in her skin and loves her glow.

D.A.D.D.

Have you seen these shirts, these D.A.D.D. shirts? D.A.D.D. stands for Dad Against Daughters Dating. The first time I saw one of these shirts, I didn't even know how to react to it, other than to stare open-mouthed until it moved out of my line of vision. I could spend happy hours telling this man all of the reasons that I do not like his shirt, why that kind of attitude is not only offensive to women but also harmful to them. I could talk to him about the importance of women being the autonomous owners of their bodies and their sexuality. But, I get the distinct feeling that this would be a fruitless and irritating venture. So instead I think about my own father and the day that he showed me his condom drawer.

When I was about fifteen years old when my father realized that in all likelihood I, his only daughter, would start having sex sometime soon. One evening, when my mother was at work and my dad and I had the house to ourselves, he showed me the drawer that he kept the condoms in—the drawer that had been shown to my three older brothers before me—and he told me this: "Here is where I keep the condoms, feel free to use as many as you need, if the supply starts to get low let me know and I will buy more of them. There are two things that you need to make sure you do. One is, that if a boy tells you he doesn't want to use a condom, you tell him that you are not going to have sex with him. The other thing is that sex is a great thing and it is something that should be enjoyed by both people, so if you are with someone and they do not care if you are enjoying it as much as they are, I would advise you to stop sleeping with them 'cause you don't need to put up with that kind of bullshit."

The next time I saw one of those fucking shirts all I could think is, I love you dad.

What If I Put Out My Cigarette on Your Face?

When I hear men use the phrase "put out" it makes me want to ask them, "What exactly is being 'put out,' your flaming penis? Yes, we'd better take care of that before the entire house burns down." Of course I know very well where the term comes from. A woman is said to be "putting out" when she performs sexual acts upon said male; "putting out her goods," so to speak. I plan to focus on the misogynist idea that women are obligated to perform sexual favors for men. Urban Dictionary has a number of definitions for the phrase, and I'd like to highlight a few exceptionally key definitions for you:

Put out: When a female dispenses her sexual favors, she is said to put out.

Ex: Joe is going to dump his girlfriend because she won't put out for him.

Put out: When a chick gives you a blowjob to fulfill your sexual needs as a man

Ex: It took her three dates but she finally put out. She gave me a blowjob, and I got to feel her up.

Sexuality could really use a makeover in our current culture, wouldn't you say? There is a huge double standard! The main issue I have with the phrase "put out," is that it pretty much takes a woman's desire to orgasm out of the scenario. It paints a picture that our bodies are meant only to please men and this is a false message to send to young men and women! Why do dudes think that we are obligated to please them? Isn't that what women's liberation was for? Hey guys, guess what? We can orgasm too; you've just been doing it wrong this whole time! Surprise! Let us make sex a cohesive act that works to satisfy both parties involved and stop pretending that women are just a screw whole with a body attached. Here is what I suggest to abolish the phrase "put out:"

#1 Ladies: DO NOT EVER USE THIS PHRASE EVER. Once you start

using it, the game is over. If you are going to use this phrase, here are the right ways to use it:

Ex: I'm super stressed with school, so I'm doing yoga to put out some positive vibes.

Ex: I'm having that wine and cheese party on Saturday so I'm thinking about putting out those vintage plates my grandmother left me when she died.

Ex: Hey look someone put out a box labeled "free stuff!" It could be puppies!

#2 If you ever hear this phrase being used by a fit, tan, hair-gelled twenty something boy, turn around and say, "Hey, listen buddy, you need to get your priorities straight! You will never be happy in a relationship until you stop pretending that you're good at sex and start RESPECTING women!"

Then hand him some condoms and say, "be safe ya filthy animal."

#3 Finally, I think the most important thing to realize is that women have amazing, powerful bodies and for our sex to be diminished to the measly two word phrase "put out" is ignorant and misleading. It's true, we are great at sex, but women need to be comfortable enough with their sexuality that they don't feel the need to use it to get things, like a fourth date with that super hot guy from work named Brad.

Our bodies are meant for so much more than sex (like dancing, being a temple for your soul, and also lifting stuff). And while women should feel liberated enough to have sex as much as they want and with whomever they want, they should also feel confident enough to not feel pressured into having sex too soon because of some male standard that turns women into sex toys.

If you are ever in an uncomfortable situation where someone is pressuring you to "put out" by cooing in your ear, "aw come on baby, put out for me please," feel empowered to laugh in his face and say, "aw baby, get a life that doesn't revolve around your dick," and then get the hell out of that situation. YOU ARE AMAZING.

The Wound that Won't Heal: Why Orange is the New Black

Have you never broken the law? I mean, at all: stolen anything, disobeyed the speed limit, did a drug, drove when perhaps you shouldn't have?

As minimal as the infraction may be, not everyone is lucky enough to escape imprisonment. I hope you never have to deal with the ramifications of the judicial system, unlike so many others, who are just like you. We must end the misconception that all convicts are deviant ... that they're bad people. They could be sitting right next to you. It could be me. Ms. 78727

Imagine this; you hear: "You have the right to remain silent. Anything you say can or may be used against you." When the truth of the matter is that it will be used against you, perhaps for the rest of your life. What you take for granted as the minimum requirements for humane living are denied during incarceration.

So, you think Orange is the New Black? Forget what you see on TV. In county jails, there are no rec rooms, no freedoms. That orange probably turned black from lack of washing. Here are some other tips about life in jail.

Do's ... and Don'ts.

DO: Take a shower. Of course, only if allowed. The men in control have no problems denying showers and/or clean clothes. (This also includes denying clean clothes if you've had the back luck of being bloodied and/or urinated on.) A shower is the only way to feel halfway clean after wearing and sleeping in the same clothes for days. Would you sleep naked with male guards checking your ID bracelet while you were sleeping?

DO: Learn to get out of the shower without exposing yourself. Good luck, since the towel barely covers your ass. Also, since the door to the ward faces the showers and male guards and male inmates enter without warning, you must learn to cover yourself while in the shower, and while getting dressed. The ethical guards holler "Cover up!" This is, of course, after they have entered.

DO: Remember that the shower is the only place you can be alone, weep, and regroup that is even semi-private. What to know about hygiene: Guards will often deny pads... for days. Hoard them. Pro-tip: learn to make tampons out of the pads.

DO: Wash your panties daily and hang them on the vent to dry. That recycled methane gas you breathe in daily works great for quick-drying clothes.

If you're denied access to the commissary, you could wear the same panties for days, months, even more. (There are exceptions: bartering, hustling, and connections all have their benefits). If you think you might go to jail, wear multiple pairs of panties.

DO: Have fun when you can. Only the men get kickballs to play with. Women can cram a roll of toilet paper into a sock for a "football." It is especially great for slamming against the wall to relieve angst. However, it will probably be taken away from you; anything not used for its original purpose is deemed contraband.

DO: Exercise. Contrary to popular belief, one does not always lose weight while incarcerated...not on two meals a day full of carbs–bologna and chips –and no recreation.

DON'T: Shut the door to your cell behind you, even for fun. The electric system is new to the jail and has glitches. If there's a glitch, you may be locked in the cell, possibly the wrong cell, which means during headcount you may not be able to make it to your room and therefore charged with escape.

DO: Ask those on the outside for books. The only books available are religious, self-help, how to be a good wife and mother, how to keep a man, and how to be a proper woman. And if you want religious books, Protestant Christianity is your only choice.

DON'T: Go to the infirmary! Medical treatment is a story in itself. Let's just say, having multiple teeth pulled without any pain reliever is unethical at best.

DO: Learn to barter and hoard. Especially the instant coffee; its like gold.

DO: Learn to use what you have. You will walk out of there like MacGyver junior. Empty soda bottles filled with hot water works amazingly for cramps, or for freezing nights. (Most nights.)

DO: Learn to be quiet in your cell. Sometimes you can tell how the weather is like outside because you can hear the rain.

DON'T: Pass kites. A kite is a letter folded and slid under the door from ward to ward. One female breaking the rules has the potential to get the entire ward on lockdown, possibly for days. Besides being locked down, this also means no visitors for anyone. You will be ostracized.

DO: Remember the following:

Solidarity. Support each other. Outside of jail women are mothers, wives, partners, sisters, and daughters; they are somebody's loved one. And when one person receives rough news, all friction is gone.

Not all of the guards are malicious; some actually care.

Tell people of the gender double-standard. Only men can be trustees, who can move freely for some odd jobs like cooking, cleaning, repairs, and passing out clean laundry. The only job women are permitted to have is washing laundry a few times a week...for a mere extra plate of food.

Not everyone gets the time for deep introspection; use it to your advantage.

DO: journal, and record inhumane activities.

DO: Plan to contact your local news. Write the ACLU.

It's been five years since I was released after almost a year of incarceration. Upon release people are thrown into the world wearing their digital scarlet letter and are unable to receive financial aid, government assistance, housing aid, welfare, social security disability, food stamps. The list goes on.

Want to get a job when you get out? I have been sought after specifically for jobs, and hired verbally multiple times…until I get the call about my background check.

Ex-convicts might be free…but not mentally. The repercussions are endless. Five years later, sitting in class, I can be flooded with shame, feeling like I don't belong on campus. The pain and shame is still here like a wound that continually breaks open with each movement I try to take.

And me? I am lucky. I was able to take that fear and determination and persevere. I had love and support not only from my family and friends, but from a few people at IUSB who knew my situation.

Now? I'm applying to graduate school in the hopes to shed light on the situation, conducting research with people who have been incarcerated. In fact, it is how I got through my days at Elkhart County Jail, telling myself I was there doing research. I graduated with many distinctions, but can still feel the wound of incarceration. Finally, though, it is starting to heal. Look around: I may be sitting next to you. You may already know me. And nobody is going to tell me I do not belong right here.

Twelve Years

Tenía 12 años. Mi apariencia era distinta a la de las niñas del colegio, no por una convicción verdadera, sino porque mi mamá no tenía dinero para comprarme el uniforme completo, así que sólo me compró el pantalón de deportes y la sudadera. Las demás niñas tenían faldas, suéteres, camisas tipo polo, etc. Mi cabello era corto, muy corto. A mi mamá no le daba tiempo de peinarme, teníamos siempre que salir con prisas a dejar a mis otros hermanos y ella a checar tarjeta, así que decidimos cortarme el pelo.

Yo era distinta, pero no lo sabía. Me gustaba pintarme los brazos a escondidas. Cuando llegué al colegio nuevo algunos vieron mis dibujos y pensaron que eran tatuajes, lo cual, obviamente, me encantó. Para la primera semana yo ya estaba agotada, esta escuela con muchos maestros y unos 30 alumnos en cada salón parecía un mundo ajeno al mío. Me cansé de las miradas inquisidoras, excepto de una.

Ella iba en el salón de a lado, en el mismo año que yo. Se llama Laura. Laura me veía como nunca me había visto una mujer. No pude reconocer qué era en su mirada hasta el día que me dijo "me gustas". Seguramente fruncí el ceo, no me acuerdo. Seguramente, mi corazón quería salir corriendo. Laura dejó un silencio y dijo "pero me dijeron que eres niña y a mí me gustan los niños". Confundida. Confundida. Confundida. ¿De qué está hablando?

En la otra escuela, donde éramos sólo 8 en el salón, 3 niñas y 5 niños, los niños me decían también "me gustas", pero yo los ignoraba, éramos amigos, jugábamos al fútbol, luchitas, trepábamos la barda, patinábamos y nos reíamos de las cosas. Nunca pensé que hubiera un límite... pero ninguna niña me había dicho algo así, normalmente yo no les gustaba a las niñas.

Cuando entendí qué era lo que Laura me hizo sentir. Cuando entendí que quería ser niña y gustarles a las niñas por ser niña... comencé a rezar. Nunca antes había rezado. Mi mamá no tenía tiempo para eso. Pero en algún programa de televisión vi que uno rezaba y se le arreglaba el mundo. Recé: Dios no me hagas lesbiana, Dios no me hagas lesbiana, ¡por favor Diosito!

Pero, o Dios no existe, o Dios no supo cómo hacerle... dieron los 13, los 14, los 15 años y yo seguía jugando fútbol con los niños, compartiendo gustos musicales, trepando bardas y llamando la atención de las niñas... ... ... todo para llamar la atención de las niñas.

Laura se volvió mi amiga y mis dibujos, tatuajes. Dejé de rezar por ahí de los 16, cuando me enamoré, y ya no quedé "otra".

Translation

I was twelve years old. My appearance was different from that of the other girls in school, not for my convictions, but rather because my mother didn't have the money to buy me the whole uniform; as such she only bought me the pants and the sweatshirt. The other girls had skirts, sweaters, polo shirts, etc. My hair was short, very short. My mom didn't have enough time to do my hair, we always had to leave in a hurry to drop off my brothers and to check her card, and so we decided to cut my hair.

I was different, but I didn't know it. I liked to secretly draw on my arms. When I arrived at the new school some students saw my drawings and thought they were tattoos, which obviously I loved. By the end of the first week I was already exhausted, this school with so many teachers and some thirty students in each classroom seemed an alien word compared to mine. I was tired of the inquisitive looks, all except for one.

She was in the classroom next to mine, in the same year as me. Her name was Laura. Laura looked at me like no woman had ever looked at me. I refused to recognize what it was in her look until the day she told me, "I like you." Surely I wrinkled my brow, I don't remember. She left some silence and said, "But they tell me you are a girl and I like boys." Confused, confused, confused. What is she talking about?

In the other school, where we were only eight in the classroom (three girls and five boys), the boys also told me, "I like you," but I ignored them. We were friends, we played soccer, we wrestled, we climbed fences, we skated, and laughed at things. I never thought there could be a limit…but no girl had ever told me something like that, normally girls didn't like me.

When I understood what it was that Laura made me feel. When I understood that I wanted to be a girl and have girls like me for being a girl…I began to pray. I had never prayed before. My mom didn't have time for that. But in some tv program I saw that one prayed and the world was fixed for them. So I prayed: "God, don't make me a lesbian. God, don't make me a lesbian, please God!"

But, either God doesn't exist, or he didn't figure out how to do it…at age thirteen, fourteen, and fifteen, I was still playing soccer with the boys, sharing musical tastes, climbing fences, and getting attention from girls…all in order to get attention from girls.

Laura became my friend and my drawings, tattoos. I stopped praying at about sixteen, when I fell in love and stopped being the "other."

Feeling Crazy

You know what sucks sometimes? Feeling crazy because other people make you seem crazy. We have to keep them a secret. We can't tell too many people...and when some people find out, they look at you differently. It's like you can hear their murmurs through their body language. They don't understand it...the daily routine of ingesting tablets in which we question their effectiveness. Everyday. I hated them. I was pissed that I was even on them. I was angry with everyone. I was upset it affected my health, and I hated being asked, "Did you take your medicine today?" if I was acting out of character. Like the medicine was supposed to just fix me. Like I was like unstable without them. It's something we all go through, but for some of us, it's extensive. 10 a.m. everyday. Refills when I'm out. Nasty taste. Sure, I'm grateful...but I still get upset, and think about stopping it.

My Mom says it's the Devil trying to test me. She's a big help. She was on them too, but hers were a lot stronger and she blacked out. Some days I mope and stay in my room. Say little...or I'll write. It's just depression...no big. Some days I just don't want to be here. Not alive...definitely not dead but like a feather or something. While you guys think I'm happy and productive all of the time, some days I'm fighting the shit out of my day—to still want to be around. I remain busy so I don't fumble into negativity or darkness. It's just depression though. But they still think you're crazy. Like they've never been there or something. You don't have to pay for my meds without insurance. You don't have to have the checkups, or hear about how you almost ate yourself alive. Yes, there are FAR FAR more ridiculous health issues and I totally respect them moreso than this, but no one talks about depression. It's real, and it sucks, and asking someone if they've taken their meds for any health issue after they're acting out of place to you is not okay. Stop looking at me like I'm crazy!

No, counseling did not always work. I'm going to get myself off of these. I'm sick of them. Fortunately, though, they helped me. A lot. But, I'm really not crazy. I'm not.

FUPA

My vagina is fat. It's soft and squishy and a little hairy right now because I've been too lazy to get waxed. My vagina is many things. It is happy, sad, angry, joyous, pink, soft, abused, pretty, ugly, squishy, and amazing, but most of all it's fat.

I think my vagina has always been fat. I dont have a lot of memory of my young vagina but for most of my life I've been fat, so I guess I'm assuming my vagina has always been fat. But until recently, I had never heard a name for fat vaginas. I mean, there are names for vaginas that have a lot of extra inner labia (Arbys vagina), vaginas that look like a sideways hamburger, vaginas that look like curtains (Meat flaps), vaginas that sort of look like flowers, vaginas that have an inner labia shaped like a heart. It could go on forever. But until recently, I had never heard of FUPA.

FUPA stands for Fat Upper Pussy Area. At first I was offended. I don't particularly like the word pussy to begin with, and now it is part of describing my fat vagina to the world? How dare someone make such derogatory remarks about my fat vagina! It's mine and you couldn't possibly understand its wonder. But after I settled down and realized it was not a personal attack on my vagina, I kind of started to enjoy it. Fupa. Fupa. Kinda fun to say. Fuuupa.

I know this seems trivial to most people, but my fat vagina has been a big part of my life. I mean, for one, its always been there. But beyond that, its being fat has always seemed special. Cause I know all of our vaginas are different and whatever, but my vagina is fun and fat.

And it's not gross. People seem to think that just because I'm fat and have a fat vagina that its not taken care of. Ignore what I said before about not waxing in a while, my vagina is almost always pristine. It smells like any other normal vagina and it is very well taken care of. And just because it's fat don't assume it's loose! Why is it that everyone thinks that? I dont have a loose vagina! My vagina is just as tight as the next girl's. Maybe tighter. Wanna know why? Because kegels are about the only exercise I like.

Did you know I've been told by men that they like my fat vagina because it hugs their penis better when they have sex with me? You know that saying more cushion for the pushin'? That saying is about my fat vagina.

So now you know all about my fat vagina: how it's glorious and doesn't get nearly enough praise as it should. So the next time you hear the word Fupa you think of that, OK?

Gendered Ads

You know what I hate? Stupid gendered commercials flashing across my television screen! I mean, I can find shit wrong with every commercial! Am I the only one who sees it? Why in the hell do you need Dove FOR MEN? Why can't it just be DOVE? In order for the man to overlook the oh so feminine dove on the soap bar, smack FOR MEN on the side! YES! I'm a man again! Yeah, baby (kisses muscle).

How about the cleaning commercials where the woman is just ITCHING to salsa with the broom or the vacuum, or to make out with a new brand of paper towel to clean up that mess her husband or her child left behind. I wish somebody would leave a mess and wait for me to clean it up. That mess, will be set right on my hubby's pillow, and where my child sits at the table. Like seriously??? And, I don't look all dolled up and in heels when I'm cleaning either. I'm in some comic book or *Duck Dynasty* boxers with some anti-color coordinated (but pretty freaking awesome) socks with zebra and jaguar prints on them...and in a tank top. Put that in your commercials, will ya?!

And what's up with the car commercials? Feel manly...blah blah blah. What if he doesn't want to drive a damn truck?!! What if he wants a smaller car? Is that NOT okay? I mean, who decided the gender of a car? Because I definitely am working on my F150, and I have a flippin' vagina!!! Can't remove her! OH MAN, and the commercial between the mother-in-law and daughter-in-law with the whole cleanest fork/spoon or whatever the hell it is. Why are they women? Because we're SO obsessed with cleaning. It's like a freakin' orgasm for goodness sake, right ladies? NOT.

I love cleanliness and organization, but that's because I was raised to clean up after my mess...not because my mother (or father) was like, "You're a woman. You must clean, Cinderella, while your brother goes to do manly things like cut the grass." Oh, I cut the grass too; enjoyed it. Lastly, we all know the hunnies do not run to a man for his oh so shiny hair, and men are not taken aback by a woman because of her oh so healthy hair. OH, one more thing, we can eat chocolates and junk food whenever we want! I have a candy stash by my bed!

Girl Card

One girl card please. What do you mean, "What's a girl card?"

Don't you have one?

One time in college my gay card was taken away from me because I didn't know who Patti LuPone was. I'd never heard the expression before, but since I sported a male body and I dated men, I assumed that the privileges to identify as such had been revoked. By an arbiter of gay.

So I'm here for my girl card. No, I don't look like you. But since when has the way that people looked been the fundamental difference between experience, identity, relationships? I'm not a girl? Then tell me. What defines "girl"?

Her body? We all start female bodied. But my mother's womb took mine away. As her androgen bath spilled over my pink, still-developing form, it stole my chance for life as a girl. Replaced my clit with this prick that defines my place in our physically gendered world. As I speak, testosterone courses through my veins. Not asking what I want. No. Just coating my face in this hair that won't come off. Deepening my voice. Flattening my chest and defiling it with hair.

So no. I don't have a girl's body. But I've always had a girl's spirit. Don't tell me you don't know what I'm talking about. I'm asking for a girl card; obviously I know what girl power is.

You see, when tracks like "Wanna Be" and "Viva Forever" first populated my CD player, my nine-year-old body wasn't much different than any other girls I knew. I was accepted. I was trusted and loved. I was also Baby Spice and my kid sister played Ginger. We'd harmonize and shake our undifferentiated bodies while watching SpiceWorld, feeling more beautiful than life itself. My body was strong, my heart felt so innocent, and my smile never looked so pretty. So you see, I've had girl power for a hell of a lot longer than this [touches facial hair]. And it runs so much deeper inside me than this [touches throat, indicating vocal cords].

Not enough for my girl card, you say? Then what else defines "girl"?

Her emotions? They say girls are more expressive in their emotions, while boys are more assertive in theirs. Well, this socially-deemed boy discovered that by expressing myself, my heart could stay safe.

In the third grade, I always left for school after a ritual.

"Goodbye, mom," I'd say as I wrapped her tight with my arms.

"I love you," she'd reply, planting a kiss on my cheek.

And one day, one god awful day, my dad decides to just push me out of the house. Before our goodbye. I'd never not said goodbye to my mom. It wasn't just the goodbye. It was her hug. That mom smell. The way just the scent of her perfume could instantly save me from my deepest worries and fears.

So when I reach my desk, tears drown my eyes. At art time, my teacher takes me by the hand as I wail, "I didn't get to say goodbye to my mom." She picks up the phone and dials my number. My mom answers, curling rollers still in.

"Hello?" she says, in that mom way of saying it.

And I say, "Mo-om."

The first thing I hear is, "Oh god, honey, what's wrong?"

"I just wanted to say goodbye to you. I didn't get to say it this morning."

"Oh bless your heart. Goodbye, sweetheart, have a good day."

My tears evaporates and my art project outshines the entire class. But twenty minutes later I'm asked to come to the hallway because my teacher wishes to speak in private. And it's MY MOM. She comes to school JUST TO HUG ME, because that is what happens every morning before school. So we hug and we goodbye. I breathe in my mom's comfort. She kisses me goodbye.

So I'm here for my girl card. I want it because then when I ride buses and answer questions, I won't seem all that strange.

"Women's studies? Why do you study women? Are you gay?"

How can I be gay if that card was revoked? The arbiter said no. He took my gay card away. Before I answer, she apologizes.

"I'm sorry, I didn't mean disrespect."

"Are you a woman?" I ask, thinking: You're okay with being you. You have your girl card.

"Do I not look like a woman?" she demands, dignity singed.

But my intent was not to challenge; if I had a card, I could tell you—tell you that I'm one of you, you're one of me.

My body wasn't always this way. I'd go back if I could. Take this hair and this chest and these balls and my name. Then by some miracle I'd be a girl, once again. I have lived twenty-four years in a body housing this girl's spirit and mind, the spirit and mind that no one sees. I'm done waiting on others to hear me out, learn my story.

What you might not realize about things like monologues is that if you give life to one girl's voice, record her pain, write her story…then people like me, sentenced to a life imprisoned within their male bodies, resonate. They scream, "Hey. Listen to her! That's just like me!"

So please, just this once. Give me the proof I deserve. I want my god damned girl card.

He Was Dying

When he called to tell me he was dying, it was the first time I'd heard his voice in many years. But his voice was familiar. Familiar so deep it was a part of me. I'd heard that voice in my crib, all through my childhood, and into the iceberg tip of my teen years. Then he left, and I was so relieved.

My father's voice had become a barometer to me over the years. I tracked it with a sea captain's diligence, determined to keep clear of his storms. If I detected a slur in his words, my heartbeat kicked up. Slurring meant the alcohol was doing its worst, drowning his inhibitions and choking his reason. Sharp words were sure to follow—words that cut and sliced. Some left a terrible sting, others an indelible scar.

He slurred his words on that rainy autumn day when he called after such a long silence between us. But it wasn't because of alcohol. It was because of tumors. Two of them, large and inoperable, had silently invaded his brain. Like homicidal squatters, he would never be rid of them, and they would never stop trying to kill him.

The damaged man who had left me damaged had received a death sentence. It was a much harsher punishment than he deserved. If the Judge had asked me for a victim impact statement, I never would have wished it on him.

All of the anger I'd felt for him over the years deflated gracelessly, and I cried. I realize now that my tears were as much for a man I hardly knew as for the father I had. I cried for the stranger with the familiar voice who was just on the verge of retirement when he learned his life was ending. It was hard to bridge the distance between that man and the one who had been my live-in dad for thirteen years. The years had created a chasm between us that neither had tried very hard to cross.

I crossed the bridge and visited him. I did my daughterly duty. Our meeting was awkward and uncomfortable. We stood face to face, recognizing the others form, but knowing nothing about each others souls; we were two strangers with the same blood in our veins. Father and daughter, as intimate as two random passengers on the morning train.

I asked him questions and received monosyllabic responses. Perhaps it was all he could muster. I don't know what to say. It echoed in my head. Perhaps it echoed in his too.

Do you want to ask me anything, Dad?

There were so many unanswered questions between us.

No.

We never grew closer during my visit. We never bridged the distance between us. Now I'll never hear his voice again, and so now my anger has dimmed, nearly extinguished. I sifted the ashes for lessons, and this is what I found.

Cherish every day. Don't put off until retirement what you could do now.

Apologize and forgive.

Fathers, don't hurt your daughters. Daughters, let go of your anger. It only burns you.

Doing Time On the Outside

As the metal gate slammed shut behind me definitively, I knew I had made my decision, I knew I could not turn back, that the natural procession of choices and consequences and life and love had all convened and that here I was in a maximum security prison walking toward an unknown fate. My mind wandered back to Isaac. Back to the man who started it all.

I met Isaac in the winter of 2009. I was immediately drawn to his caring soul, shy demeanor, and crooked mischievous grin. A story board, a kind of map wove up and down his body in the form of black and grey tattoos. I loved watching him push his sleeves up, skulls and clowns leering, the crying faces of women peeking out. He awakened something deep within me that I had buried long ago. I fell in love with a heart, not a lifestyle, not an image, not a story. I fell in love with a broken man with an amazing heart, and a derelict attitude. I loved him like none other, and I grieved him like none other. Suddenly I snapped back to reality while waiting for the second set of bars to slide open in front of me.

I paused, took a breath, and raised my head. I would not enter this environment feeling ashamed, stupid, or belittled. My eyes searched until they found their home in the face of my groom to be. Yes, I was here in this prison, in this maze of cells, tombs, and sterile hallways, a place of yelling, and dull yellow jumpsuits, K9 units, and guards with rings of keys that clanked and echoed. Suspicious looks and stares of disgust lingered, but all I could see was you, Isaac. Your eyes, your face, our future, and suddenly a peace washed over me. My mind began to wander again to a little girl prancing around wearing a white bed sheet, all tucked into place to resemble a wedding gown. Paper flowers in her hair. As a teenager that same girl fantasized about beautiful venues, bright bouquets of flowers, family members lining the aisles. Today was my wedding day, today was my slightly altered fairy tale, and I told myself that I wasn't letting that little girls dream die when I walked inside those gates, I was letting it live. In less than an hour I would be classified as a prison wife and I was ok with that.

I took my first step towards my fiance amongst the watchful eyes of inmates, visitors, guards and prison staff. I walked into the walls of this prison a thirty year old woman with a relatively normal life, yet a string of judgment always trailing her. I walked into that prison a woman madly in love with a man, a man who was incarcerated. I felt giddy, butterflies floating in my stomach just like any bride on her big day. I would be lucky though, I would be walking out of this prison a free woman. I would leave in a state of great joy and in great sadness, and I would walk out with a new label in my life because I simply loved a man, a man who lost his way and found it in crime. Yes, on Valentine's day 2012 I became the wife of an inmate. I married my husband behind three layers of steel, bulletproof glass, and bars, inside the walls of a fortress. But I had to recognize that one of the happiest moments of my life was also one of piercing loss. I walked out of those gates past the disdainful faces of many with a smile on my face and void in my heart. I had to leave my new husband behind and he would proceed to go back to his 8 ft by 10 ft cell with a hole in his heart as well.

That night we would both lay down in separate beds crying ourselves to sleep, but feeling so grateful to have found a love that even prison could not break. My fairy tale of marriage, sprinkled with the notions of society and a womans desire for the lavish of ceremony and celebration had become a prison wedding, and I was also ok with that. The ceremony was beautiful in my eyes, the grim green walls melting away to a place of safety and love. All I saw at moments were the eyes of my husband welling with tears. His eyes held me, almost in a state of protection from the despair that lurked all around us.

We were married in a tiny glass room located within the visiting room. With inmates and their loved ones watching, we said our vows, exchanged rings, and our first kiss as husband and wife. I was nervous throughout the entire ceremony, not because of getting married, but of breaking a prison rule. Could I take his hand? How many inches must I stand away from him? How many seconds is too long to kiss?

There was an adjoining glass room to ours, reserved for inmates to meet with their lawyers. A single inmate sat inside waiting for his attorney. I didn't notice him at first until his movements kept distracting my peripheral vision. I glanced behind my groom at this man. He sat one ear cocked towards the ceremony wiping the smallest of tear drops from his eyes. He stared straight ahead. In a place of hardness, of darkness of constant noise and chaos, I realized my wedding WAS important. It WAS a type of fairy tale. Isaac and I had brought a piece of humanity to a place that lacked a soul.

Isaac and I had no reception, no honeymoon, no mind blowing wedding night sex. No driving away in a car tied with soup cans as our family and friends waved us on with good wishes. Isaac's skin did not feel the starch of a suit and tie and I did not wear white. I had a simple bunch of gerbera daisies glued together by my sister so they could pass through security. When most think wedding they think catering, venue, dress, music, flowers, loved ones. Prison weddings are different. You think about whether your underwire bra will set off the metal detector? Is your dress precisely two inches below your knee? Will your simple bunch of flowers be seen as something that could be construed as contraband or a weapon? Will they cut the ceremony short because of an unforeseen lockdown?

But in the end, this wedding, this experience, this slipping from one category into another was indeed about celebration, about the beauty of peace amongst pain, about a strength of love that waits, that does time on the outside. While inmates serve sentences longer than their life spans, Isaac lives among them in his tiny cell waiting for four years to expire. Waiting for that long over due honeymoon, that uninhibited kiss with his wife. I sit staring out windows lost in thought about a husband that I cannot touch. But this marriage, this wedding was perfect in our eyes. It was our new beginning. Due to its setting, it meant something different. What really happened was this: Isaac and I shared an experience of redemption. And when people ask me the details of my wedding, I speak up with pride as a woman and a wife, a prison wife whose lavish affair was marrying the warm soul of a man in the depths of a winter. I could not ask for more. Neither could that little girl with flowers in her hair.

That Thing I Never Told You

Crawling, crawling, crawling faster
Launette's going to catch me
All is present but none to witness the disaster
Hurry, hurry, hurry she's going to tag me
The weight is enough to gag me.
I loved playing with her; she was my best friend
I twist, turn, move to bend

The couches smelled of smoke but around we crawled and played
Pinned and trapped in this dirty apartment I laid.
We were having fun with a smile and a giggle
Phil's face disturbs me as he wiggles
Grown-ups are so boring, so we're going to hide
Launnette sat staring off to the side

She'll never catch me no way
But he did behind the couch; "Stop. Get off." I don't wana play.
On top of me making funny, disturbing faces, why those faces as he sways?
She yells, "She said get off her Phil, so get off."
He pauses for a minute, reluctant I would say
My grandparents tell us girls it's time to go

But they just missed the entire show.
Sitting in the car, out the window I stare
Launette next to me but almost not even there
This heavy feeling I have inside
As if there's a monster I must hide
My clothes were on but I felt violated
Shamed, embarrassed, confused

A part of me felt bruised
It was nothing; no big deal
Then why do I feel this way I feel?
Mom about that thing I never told you
About that day I came home upset

You never would have guessed this one I bet

It's no big deal then why my frustration?
Later in life I was told he was convicted of rape and child molestation.
I'm not surprised…because there's that thing I never told you

Awake at 2 A.M.

It's 2 am. I should be asleep right now. I'm tired. But sleep doesn't come easy. I wish there was an off switch for my thoughts, because the things I remember haunt me. The memories give me panic attacks when they escape the box I put them in.

I was first abused when I was seventeen. I grew up in a religious home where "vagina" was a dirty word. My sex education consisted of "Don't do it," and "You'll go straight to hell."

Any smart parent or educator out there knows that kind of a mindset is a recipe for trouble. And mine came in the form of an older guy who showed an interest in me. I was in the middle of figuring out my body and my sexuality, and he took advantage of my inexperience. I was very uncomfortable with the things he wanted to do, but I was afraid to say no. I feared he would post photos of me all over the internet. I was afraid of getting hit. He was bigger than me, and he dominated me completely.

I went to college, and got rid of him when a new guy showed interest in me. We quickly fell in love. And I was very happy. We talked about baby names, life plans. We moved in together, and became inseparable–or so I thought.

My parents didn't approve of me "living in sin," and cut me off entirely. This blow was the start of cataclysmic depression that would deeply change me. We loved each other, but I was young and selfish. I pushed him away because of my own problems with understanding healthy sexuality. I was clingy. He responded by becoming an alcoholic in front of my eyes. He wasn't the man I gave my virginity to. He didn't tell me he loved me anymore. He cheated on me twice that I know of. He would be gone for hours at night at the bar with "friends." He avoided me. He brought strange guys into our apartment, and they would all get drunk together, ignoring me. Towards the end he would raise his hand at me, a subtle threat of violence.

I broke to my core. I sat at home, too depressed to move. This meant weight gain, and by the time I was 190 pounds, he wouldn't even touch me. He broke up with me. I lost our apartment, our dream, and the only guy I had ever trusted. I was in a really dark place. I couldn't decide if I wanted to be alive or dead. I thought I could rebound with a guy I knew around from school. He seemed like a bad boy, but I wanted some attention and to forget about my problems. The third time we hung out, I spent a whole afternoon with him at his apartment. He was my ride home, and I was in a position of vulnerability.

I told him I didn't want to take my clothes off; I told him this very distinctly. But when a girl's a little high and a lot of emotionally fucked-up, you don't have to listen to her, right? He kept pawing at me, doing more and more while I just wanted to chill. I got that disturbed feeling I remembered from the first guy. It was another guy on top of me, holding me down. It was just another guy grabbing me by the throat and calling me a dirty bitch. I tried to tell myself to enjoy it, but I couldn't. I tried to distract him with TV, video games, more drugs…none of it worked. He kept touching me.

I didn't know what to do. My parents would be furious I let a man touch me, and I couldn't ask them to save me. They wouldn't understand. I texted my now-ex-boyfriend, the only one I had ever trusted completely. I told him this guy was touching me and I didn't want it and he wouldn't listen when I said no. He told me that I should just tell the guy to stop. I had been hoping he would come in his car and rescue me from this nightmare, but he was too busy getting wasted and talking to girls at the bar to come and get me. I wasn't his problem anymore.

The nightmare finally ended when the asshole drove me home. He told me he wanted to see me two or three times a week. I ran inside my house and deleted him from all my social media sites, and never talked to him again. I figured if I deleted him from my life, I could delete him from my memory. You can't forget your past, no matter where you run. I threw myself into one or two more sexual encounters with various guys who were probably nice enough, but they just made me more miserable. I couldn't orgasm. My muscles were all clenched up, I couldn't relax, and I couldn't trust. That was my mantra. Do not trust. Do not trust. Do not trust. And honestly, who could enjoy a sexual experience like that?

I started to realize that the some of the guys I had been with hadn't been just bad boyfriends, they had been abusive. It wasn't a phrase I liked, but I realized I was a victim of sexual assault.

I still feel sometimes like it's my fault. My dad once asked me if I had ever been raped. It was an uncomfortable conversation, but it ended with me explaining how I felt like the assaults from my first boyfriend had been caused by many things. I told him there were three things that caused the abuse: The evil guys who abused me, my own mistaken trust in shady guys; and my sheltered and repressed upbringing that had made me easy prey for the first abuser.

My dad told me I was a selfish little girl for thinking that way. The abuse was entirely my fault. In his eyes, I'm a whore for opening my legs in the first place. No matter if I wanted it or not.

I want to tell myself that my dad is wrong. I didn't ask for guys to touch me where I didn't want touched. All I wanted was love. All I wanted was to have fun and be happy. But on nights like tonight, I can't sleep. I'll have flashbacks. I'll remember the words the guys would whisper in my ear. I remember how they smell, I remember the music they listened to, I remember the clothes I wore. I remember being molested, I remember having loved and lost, I remember failed hookups that make me burn with shame. That's why I'm up at 2 a.m. and can't sleep. Some memories won't go away.

Letter to Aborted Baby

Dear Someone Who Will Never Be:

First, please let me apologize for the choice I had to make. I know that given time and incubation you could have been a person, but you were in my body, and I couldn't live with myself if I made that a reality. Yes, you would have been beautiful; your father is gorgeous and I'm not so bad myself, but we are dangerous. We are mad crazy alcoholics, and any life we could have given you wouldn't have been worth living. In fact, the day I chose to get rid of you I had a fat lip he gave me for talking to a bartender, and he had a black eye for confronting me about it.

This life isn't good for anyone, especially you. I cried the whole time the procedure took place, the one that took you from me, but please understand you couldn't happen, for my life and yours, and part of me will live with this choice forever. I love you.

Your might have been mother,

Me

Low-hanging Fruit

Low hanging fruit. *Low hanging* fruit. Low hanging *fruit*. Yeah, I mean it as a metaphor. Or maybe I don't. Low-hanging fruit, ripe, delicious, sexaayy, STRONG. That's how I want to see my aging body. How do I want it to be seen? Mature, juicy, worthy of savoring. Worthy of awe. Worthy of respect.

It's not easy in a culture that hates the aging female body. I'll spare you the litany of injustice as George Clooney just gets sexier with age [rowr!], but, Golly, did you catch Meryl Streep or Gina Davis in their latest close-ups on film? Yikes! They just look OLD…Keeper-of-the-crypt old. [yech]

I'm not a fan of those cliches that try too hard, claiming that women are like fine wine, getting better with age. You can hear how hard the speaker rows against the tide of our culture. More like a tsunami, really, of cultural disgust of female bodies that lie beyond the boundaries of Cosmopolitan magazine models. Of course, we all know those bodies are airbrushed lies, but those lies get in our heads. They damage us. They fill us with shame about flesh that proves we have lived fully and well.

On my best days, I find it a relief to be aging, to be so far off the charts of culturally desirable, that I can just enjoy my body. Aging is, after all, pretty interesting. Hip bones that used to be buried in youthful flesh, now jut at angles I'm still getting used to. Hellooo, there, saucy things!

Breasts that used to sit high, well, have I mentioned low-hanging fruit? Those breasts are now as soft as late-September tomatoes, but I feel tenderly toward them. Old pals, we have seen a thing or two, haven't we? Fumbling lovers, menstrual bloat, lactating spectacles of shooting milk, a cancer scare or two. They now hang like worn flannel against my rib cage, cozy, comforting. I hope they hang around as long as I do. I know I can't count on it.

I could go on about how my youthful, curved belly used to cause me such anxiety that I spent long terrible evenings in too-tight clothes, sucking in my breath when I should have been cutting loose to Cyndi Lauper on the dance floor. Now? I've got so much post-partum flesh pooching over my underpants elastic that I can only be amused that my belly is baroque in its puckers and crinkles. How can I not feel kindly toward it, even when it swings low while I'm in a yoga move like downward dog, or when it gently slaps my partner during lovemaking? [c'mon you know what I'm talking about]

Low-hanging fruit? Sure, I feel ripe, I feel full–of experience, and love, and pain, and the throbbing pulse that reminds us we are lucky to be alive. I'm too old, happily, too old to waste any precious human energy on shame about my body. My wrinkling, surprising body is charming, sexy, funny, cozy, and ready to be appreciated, not just by others, by me, too.

Minge Hair

I love my minge hair. I love looking down at my vagina and seeing my full bodied, perky V-shaped hairball that seems to be saying, Hi, friend! I love rubbing it with conditioner while in the shower so as to make it fluffy and stylish then lie naked on my bed, twirling the mangy curly hair around and around my index finger.

I hit puberty insanely early, my breasts coming in at the tender age of 8 and my period following closely behind. My minge though, was the first sign of my woman-age. At age 7 little hairs started sprouting, and in no time, it grew into a wild, wondrous sea of dark curly twat locks. I appreciated, even loved my minge hair, but at the impressionable age of 11, my best friend accidentally caught a glimpse of my raggedy mane and acted as if it were dog shit on a rug. "You really oughta get rid of that!", she said, eyeing my minge hair with disgust, "How can you stand it having that there?"

This criticism about my hairy friend kept me up the whole night wondering, "Is it really that bad to have hair down there?" And a small voice answered, "Well, your best friend seems to think so." So when I got home the following morning, I went upstairs, found my father's razor, and set about getting rid of my now ugly, hairy friend. After I was done, I surveyed the damage, and gasped in horror. My once beautiful, full-bodied minge mane that I was so proud of, now resembled something like a bald chicken. It looked vulnerable with the plethora of red bumps scattered about it. It looked so cold and vulnerable that I truly believed that if I wiped it with toilet paper it might shatter into a thousand little pieces!

After that, I never shaved again. Soon after, I asked my friend why she chose to shave her pubic hair. Her response was matter of fact and had a "duh-everybody-knows-this" quality to it. No one likes a hairy pussy, she informed me. I wanted to know why. To this day I still do not understand the attraction to a hairless minge, and until last spring, was completely unaware of how this phenomenon came about.

Apparently long ago prostitutes used to shave their pubic hair so as not to get crabs, and in the 1980s, porn directors instructed the women to shave their pubic hair so the camera could get a closer look at their vaginas. Ever since then the War on Pubic Hair has escalated. If you ask a random teenage girl what she thinks about shaving her minge hair, she is likely to say that shaving down there is normal and a necessary sanitary, and if the subject is brought up in normal conversation and one girl admits to not shaving her pubic hair she is then subject to public ridicule. Even guys have started to shave their pubic hair. When my sister brought up minge hair, I admitted that I don't shave mine. She gave me an odd sympathetic look. Then how do you expect a guy will ever want you," she asked.

Well, I replied after a moment, I expect that a guy will want me because he finds both my personality, as well as my body, in its present state, attractive. And sure enough, two months later I started dating a guy who, when we first made love, didn't care that my minge was not shaved. He cared about me.

I don't think that I will ever fully understand why people have such visceral reactions to pubic hair, and frankly, I don't care if I ever do get it. All I know, is that at the end of the day, I like to come home, set my keys on my piano, go upstairs, take a shower, and puff up my minge.

Miss Deb Kit

I knew it had to be something bad when my mother told me to come to her room after dinner. At 10 years old, good things came at birthdays and holidays. And when good news was shared, the whole family was typically present. Why did I have to meet my mother in secret? That night I found out. Atop of one of my parents twin beds sat a long pink cardboard box. No wrapping. My mother was seated on the other bed looking unusually perky. That really made me suspicious. She had me sit next to her and started to explain that there was something called menstruation that happens to all girls.

After describing the monthly blood flow or periods, she led me over to the mysterious box labeled the Miss Deb Kit lying on the other bed. First my mother handed me two booklets to read. One was entitled, "You're a Young Lady Now." She then described how to wear Kotex napkins, pulling out the regular Miss Deb belt and the embroidered bikini napkin holder. Also inside the box were two kinds of napkins; regular and slim. It was all packaged in pink to make girls feel "dainty and feminine." I was so embarrassed when she made me try on one of the belts! The hooks and elastic felt itchy and uncomfortable. I did not want to wear this stupid thing! The pad was even worse; it felt bulky and made me walk funny.

After that awful ordeal, my mother asked if I have any questions. My initial question was sociological in focus: what about nuns? I asked. Do they get periods too? She replied that they did. As a Jewish girl I thought nuns were special and strange, and therefore in my mind would be exempt from something so messy. As a devoted fan of Laura Ingalls Wilder books, my second question was historical in nature. What about women who lived when they wore hoop skirts? Again my mother answered that these women had periods, too. Already knowing the answer, I countered with; did they have Miss Deb kits? No, my mother replied, they used rags. How disgusting, I thought. Not to be deterred, my last question was anthropological: What about the women who live in Africa and other countries where they don't wear a lot of clothes? What do they do? My mother cocked her head, paused for a few seconds and said with a slight smile on her face, I think they use rags, too!

What? I thought. Then everyone would know!

So I was right after all; it was unpleasant news. I snuck back to my room toting my big pink box, feeling a little relief knowing that I could turn to Miss Deb when the time came, and thankful that I lived in a place where I got to wear clothes!

Baby Love

I work as a postpartum nurse. When I tell people this, many say, Awwww…
I'd love to hold babies all the time. RIGHT! I care for new moms, babies
and even dads from time to time. I have seen some of the most beautiful
moments in the world, and some of the very saddest. People are struggling
everywhere, and life is hard but I know great happiness is out there. I have
cared for PTSD moms who have overcome some tremendous things. I have
seen a loving, caring mama hand her baby over to a funeral director. I have
seen moms leave their babies at the hospital to go in search of their next fix.

I have seen sunshine through the clouds on the postpartum unit. I have also
seen the ordinary everyday miracles of life. Like helping mom get her baby
latched on to her breast to feed for the first time. She looked up at me after
the baby was nursing. With a laugh and tears in her eyes she said "I did it"! It
was SO beautiful.

I remember the mom who came to meet her new baby for the first time.
With her heart in her throat, she asked a hundred questions. She must have
cried a thousand happy tears over her newly adopted baby.

The mom who is sad because she doesn't have the father's support. She is
thinking about her previous baby who didn't make it. And she is pumping
milk for her tiny baby down the hall on the Neonatal Intensive Care Unit
(NICU). She is worried if she can learn how to take care of this small person
before they have to go home.

Dads are sleeping on a pull out sofa bed, tired and desperate for coffee while
moms just need praise. They want smiles and to hear they are doing a great
job. We all need encouragement sometimes. So gosh darn it, I praise them!

I praise them for the first time diaper, even when it is hanging off the baby's
butt. I praise them for the "fumbling around" first feedings. I praise them
for walking to the NICU and pumping religiously for their sick baby. I praise
cesarean moms for walking in the halls.

I have sayings that I like to sprinkle throughout the day. "Your body carried and fed this beautiful baby while inside, now it can feed this baby outside," and, "Don't blame your breasts for rumors you have heard about breastfeeding." I am trying to create a nation of Lactivists. Our slogan will be: Everyone who CAN breastfeed, should breastfeed! I don't want breastfeeding to be a decision based on society's skewed views. They're boobs they ARE for food (and sometimes fun with a partner).

This job has sadness, anxiety, pain, excitement, joy, discomfort, wonder and miracles. The miracles and joy in the everyday are what keep me waging war against sadness and grief. I've seen it every day. I love my job, and I love what I do and it's not JUST holding babies.

I Got a Tattoo

It isn't a big thing, just a few words in my carefully, crafted script along the outside of my right foot. I got it because I had been writing the same lines of the same poem on my body for over a year in pen ink then a person I admire told me, "You should get that tattoo, and you should get it this weekend." That was a Friday, and by Sunday, the words were raised in the thin skin that stretches there, just below my ankle.

I knew that my mother would hate it. Whenever the subject of tattoos were raised, she would push her lips together and say, "They're just so tacky. No class." Those are the most un-kind things my mother can say, because they were the most unkind things her mother could say.

I warned her; I was like a guinea fowl, puffing and pruning until I was three times my size and then I called her, like I do every day.

"Mom I think I am going to get a tattoo."

She was silent, and then said, you know I don't approve. But it's your body. Considering my mother's propensity for passive-aggressive, veiled, and otherwise frustratingly hurtful wordplay, this was pretty much the best possible situation.

So I went into the shop and bit my tongue and winced as a gypsy man pushed ink into me. And then I sent my mother a picture. She replied via text:It's BIG.

Not too long after that, she called me and said that she had compiled a list of 14 mistakes that she made during my upbringing that had resulted in me getting this tattoo. I hung up and then called her back, and told her that we were going to pretend that that conversation never happened. Of course, I tell this story all the time when I'm a little drunk at parties and people ask me about the words on my foot, and here I am telling you now, so I am not doing a very good job of pretending.

The feeling I had at that moment, when I asked my mom to pretend, was the same moment I had later that year, when she told me, "I don't think that people can be bisexual. I think they're pretty much one way or the other, and either they're in a phase or pretending to be something that they're not." And I said Is this a bad time to tell you that I have a girlfriend? It's the same feeling I had when she raged against anyone who opposed our president and I asked about the drone strikes and the money for education and she began to cry and asked me why I always had to be so critical.

It is the feeling that the Greeks must have felt, watching their idols be overturned without retribution.

My mother is my most loyal fan and most devoted supporter. I love her with every inch of me, and I have never doubted that her world begins and ends with me. But she is broken, just like her mother before her, and just like me, and now I know that the fierce, unwavering love we share means figuring out how to let one another be as we are. My mother will always think that tattoos are tacky and classless. And I will always love them. And despite that, she will always love me.

My tattoo is a line from a Mary Oliver poem called Wild Geese. The first stanza of this poem is:
You do not have to be good
You do not have to walk on your knees
For a hundred miles through the desert
Repenting
You need only let the soft animal of your body
Love what it loves
My tattoo is "Loves what it loves," above all else, the deliciously, delightfully flawed woman that is my mother is what I love.

Recorded Monologue #2

Since I was a little kid, I've always been kind of feisty. I had a big brother. That always pushes you to be strong. My brother and I had such different experiences in the school system. He…he couldn't learn how to read, he was dyslexic, and no one knew he was dyslexic, and he was told he was stupid from a very young age. I was in gifted programs and I got a lot of attention, and he was one of those kids that fell between the cracks. I was told I was smart from a young age, which is good and bad. In school, it makes you weird, and that was hard. I felt outside of things.

That happened in school, where you're supposed to be there to learn…

The first day of school, freshman year, my teacher said, "We have two clocks in this classroom. One's in the front, and it's the boys' clock. One's in the back, and it's the girls' clock. And you can tell it's the girls' clock because it's a little smaller and a little slower." This is my first day of high school.

I had the same teacher junior and senior year. Halfway through senior year was the first time he mentioned a woman in the class. In a US history class. It was a small bullet in his PowerPoint that said Sacajawea, and he just said, "Sacajawea, she helped too." And moved on in the lecture.

People had told me he was very sexist and that he gave girls lower grades. But I gave him hell the entire year, and argued with him, and did it in front of everyone. One of my friends said she ran into him years later and he said, "Oh, I think about [my name] a lot, and she's a really good student." It was almost like he was pushing me in some ways, like maybe he believed in sexism, but maybe he wanted to provoke me, to provoke women.

I grew up in South Bend and I had a difficult time in high school here. I had good experiences, but I just felt like I was in opposition to everyone. One of my English teachers called me the lone voice in the wilderness in my high school. It made me stronger, made me passionate about these things, and pushed me to articulate myself. But it's painful to be the lone voice in the wilderness.

It took leaving this space, leaving South Bend, to find what I was looking for. I'm really passionate about lesbian history and women's history. I went away to a women's college and found a lot of community with feminists, so I don't feel alone anymore, but senior year was really, really hard. I feel a lot more myself now than I did in high school. I realize that I'm not the only one.

A lot of people my generation have issues with their mothers My mom and I fight a lot and we always have since I was really young. Sometimes it doesn't feel like those work/life bounds exist for her generation because they had to fight so hard in the workplace that now it's like they're still fighting. I think my generation is more about self-care. But as many fights and disagreements I have with my mom, I think she is a very strong feminist, whether she identifies with that or not. She is, and she works so hard, and she's doing really great things with her work.

South Bend has a lot of potential, and there's a lot of good people here. The women here are great women, and it's just time to rise up. That's what I learned when I left. I learned that South Bend made me a fighter.

The Glass Pillow

Dark pressure clamps down tight around my face as I inhale the brown 600 thread count pillow casing. "I am going to kill you," echoes though my ears as the fear of losing my life crawls up my spine. His arms sit heavy on my chest as he digs his elbows into my diaphragm.

Twenty-one years old. I am too young to die. Thoughts race through my brain as I see my deathbed.

Should I fight back or give in to this madness that I call my life? Three years of this shit, and I can finally put an end to it and rest peacefully. My vision starts to darken. The light hidden by my shadows finally shines through.

TRISTAN, that beautiful one-year-old little boy. I can't leave him behind to take the rage my husband hits me with every day. To take the mental blows that end the day with black and blue. I see those precious baby blue eyes that look to me for love, digging through the chaos he has endured in his short life span. It gives me the strength to fight back.

I open my eyes to the once soft pillowcase that we both picked out. It feels like shards of glass on my face. I take in what little air I can get and wiggle and fight until I can get him off of me.

"No!" I say as loudly as I can, gasping for air, "you can't kill me!"

My head is spinning as his smile comes into focus. Is he laughing? That fucking bastard is laughing.

"You're stupid," he says to me. "I was just kidding. I wouldn't kill you."

TXT MSG

A few months ago I bought a new cell phone; one that you didn't have to open up like a sea creature and that could be used for text messaging. My grown children were urging me to get with the program and start texting. They had owned many fancy phones over the years that I had paid for, eventually dropping them into toilets, abandoning them on seats of taxi cabs, or getting them stolen in coffee shops. I figured that I deserved an up-dated phone.

Coming late to the party, I decided to consult the online Urban Dictionary to buff up on my chat acronyms so I could communicate with my kids and my friends like a pro. Phone in hand, I tapped in some cute beginning phrases like:

SWAK   Sealed With A Kiss   and
SLAP   Sounds Like A Plan   and
SUL   Snooze You Lose

This was fun. I could do it. I tried a few more. As I merrily typed, in my unlimited message mode, I became quite intrigued first with the shutdown codes that my children had surely used in my presence.

AITR   Adult In The Room   or
PA   Parent Alert   like I would lurk over the tops of people's heads reading their shorthand messages.

PLZ   Please!

The number codes were equally fun and mysterious. My favorite was 831. 8 Letters, 3 Words, 1 Meaning   I Love You   Oh, how romantic!

And I liked:
404   I Havent A Clue   and
420   Marijuana   which is totally legal to text in
CO   Colorado   and   WA   Washington.
Useful acronyms I learned included

GTGP   Got To Go Pee   and

IWBAPTAKYAIYSTA   I Will Buy A Plane Ticket and Kick Your Ass If You Say That Again

WOW   Wow! I wouldn't want to send that to my boss, but I could think of a few times when it would have been the perfect response. And a few for my office mates seemed appropriate:

RUMCYMHMD   Are You On Medication Cause You Must Have Missed a Dose or

STPPYNOZGTW   Stop Picking Your Nose, Get To Work

There were some good ones that I wanted to take up as mantras for my life.
ALTG   Act Locally, Think Globally   and maybe
PEEP   People Engaged and Powered for Peace
I would be so cool sending those.

But some messaging in my inbox was a bit disconcerting. If I received the text

BBB   would I think   Bye Bye Babe   or   Boring Beyond Belief?

I found it to be quite easy to get into the not-so-secret coding of the texting world. In fact, I got a little carried away. Once I inadvertently sent the message to my friend

IAWC   If Stupid Were A Crime
She didnt text me back.
OOPS   Oops!
There was a scramble of letters that I accidently sent that confused me a bit.
TOYP   TOYP   Hmmm?
TYOP   Take-Off-Your-Pants   Take off your pants!!!
OMG   Oh My God   I'm sexting! Old ladies arent supposed to be sexting.
WTHN   Why The Hell Not?

Ooooooh, a whole new world of messaging opened up to me.
VEG   Very Evil Grin

IPN   Im Posting Naked
I now understand that I should not provoke the message
JEOMK   I Just Ejaculated On My Keyboard

OOPS Oops again.

And I knew not to answer
pws (all in lower case letters) which means playing with myself. Apparently
seasoned texters know thats not a message you should shout.

I also learned that
BANANA   Banana, the code word for penis, was not something I should
suggest on my grocery list. And
BTW   By The Way   wouldnt you know that
DEWDS   Dudes   would get a whole word, banana, not an abbreviation,
for their private part.
 ISH   Insert Sarcasm Here   Plus one of those rolling-eyes smiley faces, too.

This text messaging has really moved me forward in the techno world of
communication. The arthritis in my thumbs acts up now and again, but I will
have to say that I am beyond the cramping and I can text with the best of the
teens in the pew during church. I tweet a little and chat and blog now, too.
My kids say that if I tag them in one more photo on Facebook they are going
to unfriend me.

WGAS   Who Gives A Shit
Well, GTG   Got To Go I am off to the store to pick up the new, even
smarter, cell phone I ordered.
AWC   After While Crocodile
LOL

Mommy's Quite the Hustler

Let me tell you, a mom has many roles. But there are many roles that we take on in a single lifetime that as mommies we don't get a pat on the back for. You know those television cookie cutter mommies? The ones that bake the cookies from scratch, fold the laundry, and take their kids to soccer practice and all that good fluffy stuff?

Well I'm not one of those mommies. I bake packaged cookies, try to make sure the laundry is clean as it sits in drawers unfolded, and my daughter might have to catch a ride with a fellow player to soccer practice. I'm going to give you the real deal. I'm an urban mom, I live in Mishawaka and according to guidelines of the government, I'm poor. I say screw the government's guidelines because I am Godly, wealthy, and healthy, you hear me? Am I supposed to fit those stereotypes that come with those damn government labels? You know, poor and in rags, unclean and in section 8 housing with more kids than I can handle expecting food stamps like clockwork figuring that the Government owes me.

Well, I can say that I'm not like that and the people that I know seeking assistance only used it temporarily every time that they really needed it, which wasn't very often. I'm not on Government assistance and I thank God, that as of this moment, I don't need it. Granted, I don't have much money and that's okay because my child doesn't really want for anything more. If she does, I hustle for it. That's right, this mommy is a hustler. I do whatever I (morally) can to get my child whatever she needs and wants and if I can't get it right away, she will get it eventually.

What's a hustler? Some of you may be asking, well if you don't know let me explain. A hustler is someone who is smart in their sense of money management, using their money maker, the brain. You may think of a hustler being someone to con their way into your pockets, that's the dark side that we won't touch. A hustler is someone that is cunning, skilled and very resourceful at finding ways to make or earn money. Sound familiar? Sounds like a mom, doesn't it? I mean mothers really know how to be resourceful and stretch a dollar and even flip it to bring in more income.

Mommies like me are the REAL HUSTLERS. Myself in particular, my hustle includes my regular forty hours-a-week job and other things that could earn me money or save money. For instance I clip coupons to save an extra dollar, I donate plasma to earn some cash for my time spent there, and I consign my daughter's old clothes to buy new ones. I do eyebrows and I also do a little hair on the side. A good shampoo and condition with a nice flat iron for those who can't afford the salon at the moment. I will also babysit for the mothers who need time to themselves or can afford daycare. We women and Mommies need to stick together!

I work every day and if my paycheck isn't quite as enough, I ask for the extra hours. Sadly as a stereotypical single mother I am sacrificing that extra time that I could be spending with my daughter but a mommy has to do what she has to do even if it's something that she doesn't want to do. Are you a hustler? Let me hear all you mommy hustlers give yourself praise because there will always be things that we as mommies HAVE to do for the greater good of our children. Hustle on, moms, HUSTLE ON.

Motherhood Is Not For Me

I am a woman and yes we are the ones who give birth, but I am here to ask a question: Why does everyone assume that because I am a woman that I am going to want kids?

It has been seen that motherhood is not really a choice but rather something that is expected of every woman, something that every woman yearns for. Well, REALITY CHECK, not every woman wants to be a mother!

Hey, I like kids, don't have any problem with them but me being a mother it not want I want. So what if I don't want kids. Does that make me a bad person? Does it make me selfish?

Motherhood is terrifying to me and probably for majority of women as well. Maybe it is the fear that makes me not to be a mother, maybe it is because I do not want to be responsible for another life. Maybe I like my independence and freedom. Maybe it is a combination of all those things but what should it matter what the reason is. It is my choice and my decision and no one can interfere with that.

I like my life the way it is without kids; I do not want to give up my free time, money, and my sleep for someone else.

What about all the women who feel the same way?

Maybe all the women who don't want kids have the same reasons or perhaphs different reasons as to why they don't what children, but so be it. I want to focus on my relationship, my career, and my future.

It is okay for a man to not want kids, but the second a woman says she doesnt, it becomes a problem. Women who don't want children are looked at in such a negative way and people really think we must be crazy for not wanting kids, because who doesn't want kids right?

It is time to take a stand and stop with all the assuming that every woman wants to be a mother because who is standing up for all the ones who don't?

For the women out there who like their lives the way they are, who do not want to be responsible for another human being, we have to realize that it is okay to feel this way and there are other women who feel the same way. We as women might have the choice of whether or not to be a mother but we should not be judged if we don't want to.

The women who do not want children should not be looked down upon and we should not have to feel that something is wrong with us for not wanting children.

No, there is nothing wrong with the women who do not want children; we are just like everyone else except we do not want to be mothers. For all the women who are tired of being asked the question of When are you going to have a baby?, Isn't time ticking? Why don't you want kids?, it is time to say enough is enough.

We as women have to not let anything or anyone interfere with the decision of not wanting to be a mother.

In the end, at the end of the day, we should not have to be forced or expected to be mothers just because we are women.

My Pain, My High

Seeing red was the best part. It was my high. That cold blade would excite me in ways no one understood. I would run it through my fingers, and feel the rush take over my body. Then I would push it into my skin, deeper, deeper, until my whole hand was dripping in blood. Cutting has been my addiction, my drug of choice. My hatred for my body and for myself turned me into my own punching bag. The first time I had sex, two weeks shy of my sixteenth birthday to a complete stranger in a hotel room, and my first threesome by the age of sixteen with my boyfriend at the time and his best friend, because hey, you want me to like you still, right?

By the age of seventeen was when my hatred for myself hit its all time low, my first time with three men. I remember looking at my young, naked, and no longer innocent body, and I hated it. We put so much emphasis on first in our society, our first kiss, our first love. So I cut my body, out of anger, out of self-hatred, and out of feeling like I had lost control over me. My inside was searching for love, for affection, something I longed for as a teenage girl, and I thought by giving away my body that I would feel this, but I felt nothing but shame and emptiness. So I cut to feel something, to feel anything other than the guilt, the loneliness, and the utter disgusting feeling I felt for MY OWN BODY. It's been nine years, and I still struggle with my craving for my addiction, but after seeing a counselor, I no longer see red. I realized that giving away my body was not love, and my scars that I see every day are my reminder that this is MY BODY, the only one I get, and I have to respect it, for ME.

My Sweetest Aunt Nala

I thought about you the other day when I received a pin for one of my awards and even last semester during my awards ceremony. I think of you often. Your laugh over the phone–a laugh so loud we had to take the phone away from our ear. Actually, we could hear your laugh from the other room...while you were on the phone...WITHOUT being on speakerphone! I remember how excited you were to see what I'd looked like after I'd grown up...my brother too. I remember how you wanted every picture of us from Facebook. You'd say, "Ohhh giirrrlll! You look just like your Mom! I bet you're as crazy as she is too!" I remember you reading my poetry-all of my poems.

You were the only aunt of mine that did. Besides Mom, my brothers, and Papa K, no one else took the time to learn about my dreams-even cared about them. You loved my poetry. I remember the plans you had with Mom helping kids. You wanted some. I remember Mom telling me your husband and his family mistreated you. I remember your love for wine. I remember your emotional drinking. I remember Mom asking you to stop. I remember the diets, alcoholism...I've learned about your abusive lover. I know you loved us. I loved you too. I remember us talking about me visiting before it happened. I was going to come. I promise. I remember the call in class...and the headache I got from crying. Mom cried too.

I remember promising you a copy of the book my poem was in. I didn't get to give it to you...but I had it. For you. You won't get to read another poem. I won't hear your laugh again. Mom won't have one of her great friends physically, and you won't be at my graduation, but for any award I do receive, I'll have a seat saved for you. Every time. Congestive Heart Failure...alcohol consumption. You're never forgotten, but I'm glad you're not suffering anymore. You're loved.

Honestly, I don't really want pity for my story. I want people who have the opportunity to take care of themselves to do just that. Be aware of your health. Make wiser decisions...and if you need help, please get it. Because someone, somewhere loves the shit out of you. You're not unnoticed.

On the Mat

Inhale,

Standing at the top of my yoga mat, I glance around the room hoping not to make eye contact with anyone in the class. But all eyes are on me!

I am heavier than most; ironically, my weight makes me feel inadequate when I am wearing fitness clothing.

My flexibility is limited and contributes to my feelings of judgment from others. I CAN touch my toes, my heels DO reach the floor in Down Dog, but I am not able to come into a full wheel or handstand pose. I guess everyone needs a goal, right?

Along with the lacking body image, I suffer from directional dyslexia. I know my right hand from my left, but something happens when I attempt to reverse the directions. Laughing it off, I attempt to move on.

I try not to take myself too seriously. After all, it is just a yoga class. We are not mediating or worshipping a deity, just physical fitness, increase my flexibility and reduce my stress level.

Occasionally, I feel more stress after a yoga class than before! At times, I feel challenged by others to work harder and faster to be accepted by them. Little do they know, my self-esteem is about as thick as my thin yoga mat. I thought yoga was supposed to be peaceful and loving, not judgmental.

Not too long ago, I thought about screaming in the middle of warrior one, "I am done with this!" and slamming the door as I left. Maybe then they would take me more seriously.

I am not vegan, or even a vegetarian. My car, which is not a Prius, doesn't display a Namaste sticker. Let's face it; I am not your typical yoga teacher.

Exhale.

Mom's Sick

When my mom got sick, I got to know her better than I ever had before.

Once my siblings and I realized that the chemotherapy wasn't working, we called in hospice. We took over her care at home and I spent four days a week with her. I paid her bills, changed her bed with her in it, and cooked her meals while I was there. I even had to change her diaper and bathe her. It seemed I was always cleaning, doing laundry, going to the grocery store, and doing other various chores.

There were days when she was the mom I had always known and days when she didn't even know who I was.

One day after she had eaten lunch and the dishes were done, we were watching TV, and she looked at her feet and said, "Painting my toenails always makes me happy."

So I painted her toenails. And I kept painting her toenails. Even when the hospice nurse told us that the end was near, I painted her toenails one last time, knowing she would have painted toenails for all eternity.

Now, as I am sitting here missing my mom so much I could cry, even though it is cold and snowy, even though I know that I won't be wearing sandals any time soon and no one will see them, I am painting my toenails, and it makes me happy.

Two Spirit: My Journey Home

Two Spirit is my gender. My Two Spirit identity informs how I interact with other Indigenous folks, guides how I engage with the world at large, and most importantly it influences how I experience, and am in relationship, with myself.

To be Two Spirit is first and foremost to be Indigenous, connected to Native culture and rooted in Indigenous histories. Two Spiritedness–is foundational to the histories of Indigenous societies, it informs our present day experiences, and with the resurgence and reclamation of traditional Indigenous teachings, Two Spirit identities also move with us to shape our futures. My Two Spirit identity places me at the intersection of the LGBTQ community and Indigenous culture, which is a unique place to be.

Being Two Spirit means placing oneself within an Indigenous worldview that is altogether different than the colonial European society that has grown up around us. The Indigenous worldview is one that centers on gender expression and identity, not sexual orientation. The labels and concepts just don't line up!

The term "Two Spirit" is a modern term coined as a way to have common language across the Two Spirit intertribal community. Each tribal society has its own words for Two Spirit identities - within the context of that culture.

Not every indigenous person who uses the term Two Spirit, is naming their gender identity. For some of us though, to be Two Spirit is to navigate gender, in a wholly Indigenous way. Two Spirit is a gender identity where both masculine and feminine spirits coexist in one being. Each Two Spirit person experiences and expresses their identity uniquely. Some of us were born with "girl parts" some with "boy parts." An Indigenous person of transgender experience may identify as Two Spirit, but Indigenous lesbian, bisexual, and gay individuals may also identify as Two Spirit. There is space here–in the Two Spirit realm–for Indigenous genderqueer, gender non-conforming, and other non-binary indigenous folks. Some of us are butch, some femme, and some androgynous–but the common threads we share, are our queer identities and our Indianness.

Before the European invaders hit the shores of the Americas, the emphasis in tribal societies was not on placing people into categories, it was about empowering the individual to fulfill their role in tribal society. There was a flexibility that enabled individuals to express their particular gifts in community. As a result, Two Spirit people often performed sacred ceremonial and spiritual functions reserved specifically for them. Tribal societies honored their Two Spirit people.

Despite what you may have heard, there is no one way to be gay, no official lesbian "lifestyle," and no bi-laws for the bisexual. Gender is unique and complex for everyone—and the Indigenous worldview makes space for these realities. Likewise, there is no single Two Spirit identity. Different experiences of Two Spirit identity are simply understood as different ways of being Two Spirit.

I can only speak to what the term Two Spirit means to me, and the way I experience my Two Spiritedness. There is an innately female spirit within me, and an innately male spirit within me. They coexist. They are a team. They work in consort to inform what I do, how I walk in the world, and how I breathe from moment to moment. But, in the place where they come together deep in my innermost core, they have grown together; they are woven and twisted around each other in an entirely beautiful way. The interconnectedness, the depth and rhythm of my Two Spirit identity has taken me to deeper understandings of myself. Two Spirits—one solidly rooted core.

Revealing these aspects of my identity has been like scrubbing an old tile floor with a toothbrush and uncovering a fiercely beautiful mosaic. Each individual tile of understanding that is revealed contributes to my overall image of self.

In indigenous circles, beginning to walk a Two Spirit path, is not a process of coming out, so much as a process of coming in. Coming in—to our cultural and ancestral home. Coming in—to a deep understanding of the ancient histories and traditions associated with our Indigenous gender identities. Coming in—to the warmth of our cultural fires—and finding nourishment there, finding home.

When I initially used the term Two Spirit to self-identify, it was a way of affirming both my identity as a member of the LGBTQ community and my Indigenous identity.

Now I identify as Two Spirit. I claim Two Spirit as my gender—not male or female, but an ancient non-binary gender identity uniquely and wholly Indigenous.

This Two Spirit journey of self-discovery has been my journey home.